Cities of the Revolution

CHARLES TOWN

By Susan & John Lee

Illustrated by Phil Shaffer

 CHILDRENS PRESS, CHICAGO

Library of Congress Cataloging in Publication Data

Lee, Susan.
  Charles Town.

  (Cities of the Revolution)
    1. Charleston, S.C—History—Revolution,
1775-1783—Juvenile literature. I. Lee, John, joint
author. II. Shaffer, Phil, ill. III. Title.
F279.C457L43   917.57′915′033   74-23361
ISBN 0-516-04685-3

1 2 3 4 5 6 7 8 9 10 11 12 R 78 77 76 75

CONTENTS

In a revolution, people from the same country fight each other. A revolution is always a sad war. Good friends find they are no longer friends. Families are broken up if a son or brother joins the other side.

This book tells about a city and its part in the revolutionary war between England and her 13 colonies in America. The Americans won, but it was a sad war between two peoples who were once one country.

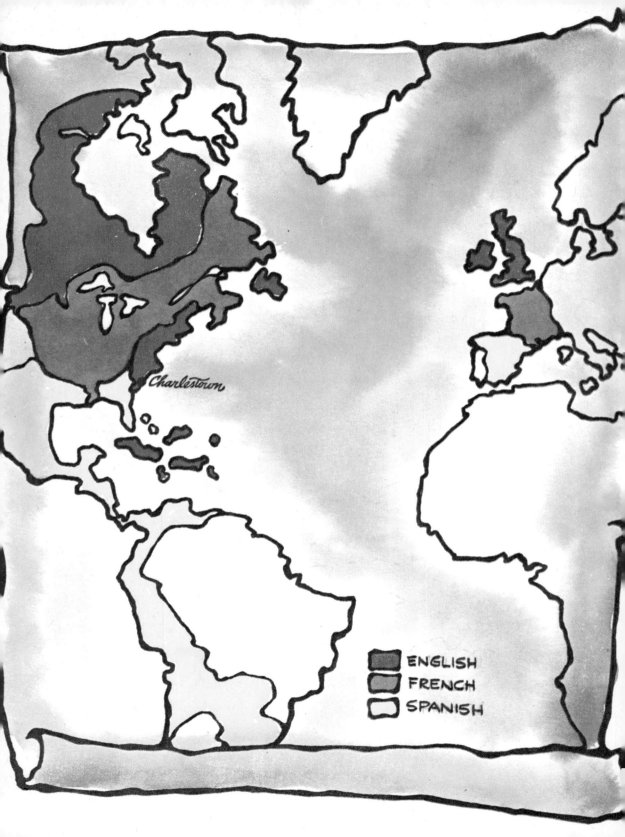

Charlestown

ENGLISH
FRENCH
SPANISH

Chapter 1

THE ENGLISH OF CHARLES TOWN

The first English families came to what became Charles Town in 1670. That was over 300 years ago. At that time, only Indians lived along the rivers and in the woods.

People in any new colony face many problems. How will they get their food? Is there good, clean water to drink? What will grow in this new place?

Where is the best place to build the new town? What can they use to build houses and stores? Will they need to build a fort around the town? How cold does it get in the winter?

The woods along the rivers were full of good trees for building houses. There were deer and birds for food. There were fish and oysters in the rivers and the harbor.

The summers were hot and the winters were cool. Cows and pigs did not need barns in the winter. The soil was rich, so the farming was good.

There was money to be made in farming and trading. Life was good for the English colonists in Charles Town. In colonial days, a good life was hard to find. So more and more people moved to Charles Town.

Two big rivers flowed into Charles Town Harbor. One was named the Ashley River. One was named the Cooper River. The first homes were built on the west bank of the Ashley River. Then the town was moved to the east side of the river. Finally the town was moved to a dry place on the Cooper River.

The river was deep in front of the town. Ships could sail up to the new docks. Some people moved up the rivers. They started their farms along a river. In some places they built new towns.

A tall wall went around three sides of early Charles Town. The wall made the town into a fort. There were cannon at the four corners of the town. There were two drawbridges at the gates to the town. There was a low wall along the river. There was a small creek, or river, in the town. This was the place where people could get water. Some people lived on farms outside the town. In the early years there was fighting with Indians or pirates. Then the farmers could go into the fort to be safe.

Chapter 2

CHARLES TOWN GROWS

By 1708, there were about 9,000 people in South Carolina. About 4,000 were white. Of the whites, 950 men made up sort of an army. They had guns and leaders. It was their job to fight if the colony was attacked. There were about 4,000 black slaves. There were about 1,000 Indian slaves.

In the next 70 years, Charles Town grew fast. There were almost 11,000 people there. South Carolina had 124,000 people. Why did these people come to this colony? There were many reasons.

One reason was Charles Town's fine harbor. Ships were safe in the harbor. This was one of the best places in America for trade.

One reason was the rich farm land and the good weather. Crops were easy to grow. The cows, pigs, and horses didn't need winter barns.

One reason was the freedom people had to follow their own religion.

There was one reason we know today was a bad reason. South Carolina believed in slavery. One black man was known to be working in Charles Town in 1670. Two years later, the first shipload of slaves was brought in from the West Indies. For many years, many black men and women were brought from the West Indies or Africa.

These slaves were owned by whites. They did
much of the hard work in farming. These slaves
did not have any kind of freedom in South
Carolina.

The slaves worked the land owned by white colonists. There were two main crops—rice and indigo. A Dr. Henry Woodward got a special bag

of "golden" rice from a ship captain. The rice had come from an island off the east coast of Africa. The rice grew well along the Carolina rivers.

A young woman farmer, Eliza Lucas, started to raise indigo. The leaves of this plant were used to make blue dye. The English and French used indigo to dye cotton cloth blue.

Rice and indigo were the crops that made many farmers and planters rich. At harvest time these crops were put on flat boats and sent down the river to Charles Town.

At the town, the crops were stored in warehouses. Then they were loaded on ships to be sent to England. There the crops were sold for food.

Long docks stood along the Cooper River. The traders had stores and warehouses along the street by the river. Ships came to Charles Town from England and the West Indies. A few ships came from the other English colonies. This sea trade meant good jobs for many men.

South Carolina also sent deerskins, furs, and wood to England. England sent tools, guns, and clothing to South Carolina.

South Carolina sent food, wood, and Indian slaves to the West Indies islands. The islands sent back sugar, rum, and black slaves. A number of goods were traded with the other colonies.

Trade was good for Charles Town. It made money for the traders. It made money for the farmers. It made money for the men who owned the ships. It made money for many traders in England who sent goods to the colonies.

Chapter 3

GOOD AND BAD TIMES

Not everything about life in South Carolina was good. There were wars with the Indians. There was fighting with the Spanish from Florida. Sometimes only a few people were killed. Sometimes many were killed.

There were hurricanes that knocked down houses and stores. Once, much of Charles Town burned down in a fire. There were years when many people died from smallpox or yellow fever. Sometimes everyone in a family would die from sickness.

The early part of the 1700s was a fine time for pirates. The English and French captured Spanish ships. The Spaniards and French captured English ships. The Dutch and English captured French ships. It seemed as if everyone was out capturing someone. The ships were full of gold, fur, and slaves. Whoever captured them made a lot of quick money.

Then the countries agreed not to capture each other's ships. Now the pirates went to work for themselves, instead of some country. English pirates captured English ships. And English pirates began to capture ships from the colonies.

One of the pirates who bothered Charles Town the most was Stede Bonnet. He was a gentleman planter from the West Indies. Then he went into the "business" of piracy. In 1717 he captured

two ships outside Charles Town Harbor. In 1718 Bonnet and Blackbeard captured nine Charles Town ships. Bonnet sent a message to Charles Town. The town had to send him a load of medicine. If they didn't send the medicine, he said he would send them the heads of some people he had captured. Charles Town sent the medicine, and Bonnet sailed away.

The people of Charles Town knew they had to do something about the pirates. They fixed up two ships, the *Henry* and the *Sea Nymph*. Each had eight guns and held about 70 men. A Colonel Rhett was in charge of the ships. He found the pirate ship, the *Royal James*, up a river near Cape Fear. The ships got ready to fight, but all three were stuck on a sandbank. The *Henry* and the *Royal James* were like two small forts. They shot at each other for about five hours. At last the ships got off the sandbars. Charles Town's ships captured Bonnet's ship. The pirates were taken back to Charles Town. In time, all but four were hanged.

Later another pirate fleet showed up outside the harbor. The people of Charles Town fixed their little navy to look like trade ships. They even used the *Royal James*. They sailed out of the harbor and let the pirates catch them. As the pirates came close, the Charles Town ships began to fire on them. Again the pirates were beaten! The captured pirates were taken into town and hanged. From this time on, the pirates left Charles Town alone. They stayed away from places where the people were willing to fight.

There was one very strange thing about the battle. One of the pirate ships had 36 women locked up. They had been on their way from

England to Virginia when the pirates captured them. The women were saved by the fighting sailors of Charles Town.

Yet, even with wars and sickness, people kept coming to the colony. There were jobs and money to be earned.

Most of the people who came were poor. In England, most people didn't own land. In the colony they had a chance to own their own land. They could build their own houses.

If they worked hard, they could save a little money. They could buy cows and pigs. They could sell their crops and meat. They would save this money from trading. Then they would buy a slave or two. With the slaves, they could farm more land.

Charles Town had many good stores and markets. There was a fish market near the river.

There was a meat market at the corner of
Church and Broad streets. There were sweet
shops and coffee shops. There was a theater for
plays.

There were good furniture-makers in the town. They made beautiful chairs and tables. There were silversmiths who made cups and dishes. There were soapmakers and candlemakers. There were shoemakers and tailors. Most of these people had a store on one floor and lived above it.

There were blacksmiths who made tools and fences. There were shipbuilders and sailmakers. There were men who made barrels by the hundreds.

Charles Town was a city of beautiful homes. Some were made of brick, but most were made of wood. Many houses had fine iron fences and gates.

These good stores and homes made Charles Town a good place to live. But trouble was coming to South Carolina. And the trouble would be with the old mother country, England.

Chapter 4

THE RIGHTS OF
ENGLISHMEN

South Carolina belonged to England. The King of England sent a governor to run things in South Carolina. The governor was almost always in trouble. He had to see that the colonists lived by the King's laws. He also had to help the colonists get more land and build more towns. Sometimes the colonists wanted to do things their own way.

More and more the colonists began to think of themselves as Americans. They wanted to make their own laws. They wanted to have their own taxes. They wanted to run their own towns.

At the same time, the colonists wanted help from England. They wanted help when the pirates came. They wanted help with the Indians. They wanted help in their fights with the French or the Spanish.

England sent ships and soldiers to help the

colonies. England sent guns and bullets, cannon and powder. England paid for these things and for the war. But England wanted its colonies to pay part of the cost of these wars.

England put taxes on paper and tea and other things sold in the colonies. The colonies had to buy these things from England. But they didn't like these taxes.

England said it had the right to tax any English colony. The colonies said they had not voted for the taxes. In England, people voted for the men who were members of Parliament. The members of Parliament voted on all taxes for England and its colonies. The colonists didn't like any tax that had to be paid in the colonies but not in England. The English colonies said that Parliament was taking away rights that *all* English people had.

The colonists said, "We are English!" So the colonies have the right to vote for members of Parliament. Or, the colonies have the right to vote for members of their own Parliament to be held in America.

"No," said the King and his Parliament. Colonists don't live in England. They live across the ocean in America. We will make your laws and vote on your taxes.

Then 12 of the colonies voted to hold a Congress of their own. Congress was the word Americans used for Parliament. Each of the 12 colonies voted for the men it sent as members of this Congress.

The first Congress was held in Philadelphia. The members of this Congress said they could vote on taxes for the colonies. They voted to start their own army. And they said they would obey the King of England but not his Parliament.

Things got worse between England and the colonies. There was fighting. On April 19, 1775, English soldiers and Americans were killed at Lexington and Concord in the Massachusetts colony. The Americans put their army around Boston.

South Carolina heard news of this fighting. The South Carolina Congress voted to start its own army and navy. The navy captured some English ships full of powder. A ship full of powder and food was sent to the American army around Boston.

The American Congress met again in

Philadelphia. An American army was sent into Canada. Then came battles on Bunker and Breed's hills outside Boston. Many more English and American soldiers were killed. Congress made George Washington the General of the American Army.

Many Americans didn't want a war. The Congress told the King that the colonies were still loyal to him. The Congress told the colonies *not* to say they were free of England.

Some members of the English Parliament didn't want a war. They tried to get Parliament to say the colonies could have their Congress. But the Parliament voted *no* to this. It voted to say the colonists were rebels and at war with England. The King said the same things.

On June 1, 1776, some 50 English ships sailed up to the sandbar outside Charles Town Harbor. War had come to South Carolina.

Chapter 5

THE AMERICANS OF CHARLES TOWN

A small English ship sailed carefully along the sandbars. It marked the places where there was deep water between the sandbars. Then 11 English warships sailed into safe water a few miles from Charles Town.

These English ships had not come as friends. Many of them carried tough English soldiers. The King's warships had come to show South Carolina that it was still an English colony.

The English warships could be seen from Charles Town. Some men climbed to the top of tall buildings. They used spyglasses to count the cannon on the ships. The two biggest warships had 50 cannon each. There were five more warships, a bomb ship, and three other ships. All together, the 11 English ships had 270 cannon.

The English sent 2,000 soldiers to Long Island. Then they sailed their warships close to Sullivan's Island. If they could get by Sullivan's Island, they could attack Charles Town.

The people of Charles Town talked about the English plans.

"They are going to attack Sullivan's Island."

"Sure they are. They will send their ships in close and attack the fort with their cannon."

"Right! Then they will send their soldiers from
Long Island to land on Sullivan's Island."

"If they take Sullivan's Island, then they can
sail up and attack Charles Town."

The Americans had put their cannon in three places. Some were at the waterfront in Charles Town. Some were on James Island. Some were in a fort on Sullivan's Island.

The fort on Sullivan's Island was built of palmetto logs. There were two rows of logs, 16 feet apart. The space between the logs was filled with sand. There were 435 soldiers and 31 cannon in the fort.

On the morning of June 28, 1776, the English sailed near the fort. They began to shoot their cannon. The Americans soon saw the fort was a good one. The English shells went through the soft logs and blew up in the sand.

The English warships were hit again and again. The captains of both big ships were badly hurt. Sailors fell dead or hurt. The sails were full of holes. Cannon balls knocked holes in the sides of the ship. Three ships got stuck on a sandbar.

The English soldiers tried to wade over to Sullivan's Island. But the water was too deep. That attack stopped. But the English ships went on firing. The English were brave men even when they were losing. The fighting went on until it was dark. Then the English sailed away from the fort.

Only 12 Americans had been killed. The English had over 200 killed on their ships. One ship had been blown up. It took the English five weeks to fix their other ships. On August 2, the last English ship sailed away.

On that same day, the people of Charles Town heard the news about the Declaration of Independence. All 13 colonies had told the English they were free and united states.

Chapter 6

WAR AGAIN, THEN PEACE

For the next three years, Charles Town was at peace. Then English soldiers landed in Georgia. They beat the Americans there and moved into South Carolina. More English soldiers came, until there were 14,000 of them. The Americans in Charles Town had 5,000 soldiers.

This time the English moved with great care. They landed on John's Island. They blocked the harbor with their ships. They crossed the Ashley River and dug in above the town. There was no way out of Charles Town for the Americans.

The city held out for almost a month. The English soldiers moved closer and closer to the town. The English cannon began to knock down houses and stores. Part of the town was set on fire. Many people were killed or hurt. When they were almost out of food, the Americans gave up.

The English captured the city. They captured almost 400 cannon. They captured almost 5,000 American soldiers. They captured many barrels of powder and other supplies. It was a great battle for the English to win.

The English put the captured soldiers in old ships. They did not feed them well. Many of the men became sick. Many American soldiers died in the jail-ships.

The English put the American leaders into jail. The town was run by the English and by Tories. Tories were colonists who had stayed loyal to King George.

Life became very bad for the wives and children of American rebels. They didn't have much food. They had to live in small shacks. They had no good ways to earn money. Many women and children became sick and died.

The English began to capture other towns in South Carolina. The English won all the big battles. But the people of South Carolina never gave up.

There were three great generals from South Carolina. They were Francis Marion, Thomas Sumter, and Andrew Pickens. They didn't have many soldiers. But they kept the English mixed up most of the time.

These soldiers would hit the English hard. Then they would move back. They kept the English from getting food. They kept the English from getting horses. For the English, it was like trying to fight bees. They could win the battles, but they couldn't win the war.

Then two other generals came down from the other states. They were Daniel Morgan and Nathanael Greene. None of these American generals won any great battle. But they drove the English wild. They hit and ran. They made things so bad that the English moved north into Virginia. These five generals, with their little armies, drove the English out of the Carolinas.

There were still many English soldiers in Charles Town. The Americans put a small army outside the town. They couldn't get in. But the English couldn't get out.

The war ended at Yorktown, Virginia. The Americans and French captured the English army in the south. There were still a few small fights, but the war was over. Many Americans had died. Many English had died. Now the 13 colonies were truly free states. They were free because some men were willing to die for those states.

On December 14, 1782, the English flag came down in Charles Town. The American soldiers came into town as the English left. Over 4,000 Tories and 5,000 slaves sailed away on 300 English ships. Now the state was free of English rule.

After the war Charles Town had to rebuild many houses and stores. Soon, the town became a city. It still had its great harbor. The farms began to grow good crops again. More people came to live in the city and the state.

Before long, the traders and farmers began to make good money again. The town had won one great battle and lost one. At peace, the city won its greatest battle. It again became a great place to live.

Charleston Chamber of Commerce

AUTHOR'S NOTES:

Up to the Revolution, the town was called *Charles Town*. During the war, both Americans and English began spelling it *Charlestown*. In 1783, the "w" was dropped and it was called the city of *Charleston*.

At first, Carolina was one colony, Virginia was to the north. The Altamaha River (in Georgia) was the southern boundary. South Carolina became a colony in May, 1719. North Carolina became a colony in July, 1729. Georgia became a colony in 1732.

Charles Town was the capital of Carolina until 1712. It was the capital of South Carolina until 1790. In that year, Columbia, in the center of the state, became the capital,

The tip of the peninsula between the Ashley and Cooper rivers was called White Point or Oyster Point. The name came from the white oyster shells piled up on the point.

Rivers were the main roads of South Carolina for years. When an area was settled, people said they were "seating a river."

The early planters made large canoes from cypress trees. A canoe was *rowed* by 10 or 12 men. It could carry 50 or 60 barrels of rice.

Many of the early houses were called "single houses." They were one room wide so the wind could blow all the way through the house in the hot summers. Later, "double houses" had a long hall for the wind. There were two rooms on each side of the hall. About 1740, the first floor of houses were used for business. Families lived above the stores. The stairs were outside in gardens at the back of the store.

There wasn't much stone along the rivers, so most houses were built of wood or clay brick. The bottom wall, or foundation, of buildings was made of tabby. Tabby was concrete made of oyster shells.

St. Michael's Church still stands at 80 Meeting Street. It was begun in 1752. The first services were held in 1761. The steeple, 190 feet high, was the tallest place in town during the Revolution. Its bells came from England in 1765. The English soldiers took them to England in 1782. They were sent back later and still ring today.

In the summers, many people fell sick from yellow fever, typhoid, or malaria. It was said the colony was paradise in spring, hell in summer, and a hospital in the fall.

The part of South Carolina *away* from the ocean was fairly well settled by 1756. Many settlers came down the mountain valleys from Virginia and Pennsylvania. These settlers were said to have come into the colony "by the back door." Many were cattlemen. They used long, cracking whips and were called "crackers."

In 1770, the streets of Charles Town were not paved. Some streets had crushed oyster shell sidewalks in front of stores and houses.

There used to be an old Watch House at 122 East Bay Street. Pirates were held there before they were hanged. Later the Exchange House was built there. In 1775, the South Carolina Congress met there. After the English took Charles Town, they used part of it for a jail.

By 1775, there was a Main Post Road, used by horsemen, from St. Augustine, Florida to Montreal, Canada. From Florida the road went along the coast through Georgia, South Carolina, North Carolina, Virginia, Maryland, Delaware, Pennsylvania, and New Jersey to New York City. From New York the road went up the Hudson River and into Canada. From New York there was a Boston Post Road that went through Connecticut, Rhode Island, Massachusetts, and New Hampshire to what is now Portland, Maine.

The fort on Sullivan's Island was named Fort Moultrie after Colonel Moultrie beat the English in 1776. The fort was rebuilt of brick in 1811. It still stands.

One hero of Sullivan's Island was Sergeant William Jasper. The English shot down the flag on the fort. Sergeant Jasper jumped down, got the flag, tied it to a cannon sponge, and put it up again. All this time the English cannon were firing.

After winning at Sullivan's Island, the soldiers were given two flags. One was red, the other was blue. On each was a coiled rattlesnake and the words, "Don't tread on me." One of these flags was shot down at a battle for Savannah. Sergeant Jasper again jumped out and got the flag. But as he climbed back to put it up, he was killed by the English.

After Charlestown was captured, black slaves who belonged to rebels were rounded up. The English took them to the West Indies and sold them.

When the English left Charlestown in 1782, many English and Hessian soldiers hid in the town. They wanted to stay and become Americans. The English took about 4,000 American Tories with them. They also took about 5,000 blacks. The blacks thought they were going to be free. The English officers sold them again as slaves.

In 1783, Charlestown was in ruins. Many houses had been burned. Many had been hit by cannon balls and shells. The English robbed the houses before they left. They even took the church books and bells from St. Michael's Church. Farms and plantations had been burned. The horses were dead. The cattle had been eaten. Many rice fields had dried up. People had small gardens, or many would have starved.

By 1793, the city and the state had been rebuilt. The plantations were growing rice and cotton. Many ships came to Charleston's Harbor. Business was good. The state had recovered from the war.

SOME DATES ... SOME FACTS

1663	King Charles II gave Carolina lands to some of his friends.
1666	English discover the harbor where Charles Town was later built.
1670	First colonists came to what became South Carolina. There were 160 men and women who settled on nine acres at Albemarle Point, later called Charles Town after Charles II.
1672	There were 263 men able to bear arms (be soldiers), 69 women, and 59 children under 16 years old. In July, a town was marked out by Oyster Point along the Cooper River. It was laid out west to what became Meeting Street, south to Water Street, and north to Broad Street.
1680	Most people moved to Oyster Point and called it Charles Town. The old Charles Town was then called Old Town Plantation.
1682	St. Phillip's, the first church, was begun at the southeast corner of Meeting and Broad streets.
1684	First trouble with pirates.
1685	Presbyterians built their "White Meeting House," which gave the name to Meeting Street.
1691	Rice became a major crop on plantations along rivers.
1697-98	Many people die from smallpox.
1699	Hurricane damages the town. Many die of yellow fever.
1708	There are 9,580 people in the colony. There were 4,080 whites. There were 4,100 black slaves. There were 1,400 Indian slaves. The army had 950 white and 950 black men.
1718	More trouble with pirates. Many were caught and hanged.
1721	First newspaper was the *Gazette.* It was sold every Saturday.
1723	Second St. Phillip's Church built on Church Street. St. Michael's Church was built in 1752 on place where first St. Phillip's had been.

1738-39	Many people die from smallpox and yellow fever.
1740	Fire burned half the town in four hours.
1743	There were 30 black children in a missionary school.
1752	Hurricane damages the town.
1770	There were about 11,000 people in Charles Town, and about 124,000 in South Carolina.
1774	July 7. Over 100 delegates from all parts of South Carolina met at Exchange House. They elected the five men who went to the First Continental Congress.
1775	March. The American rebels steal guns and gunpowder from the English.
1775	May 8. The news of Lexington and Concord arrives in Charles Town. A ship from Salem brought the news.
1775	June 4. South Carolina is first colony to set up a government independent of England.
1775	September 15. South Carolina troops take over Fort Johnson from five English soldiers.
1775	November 11. English ship, *Tamar,* and South Carolina ship, *Defence,* fire at each other but no one is hurt.
1776	January 10. South Carolina starts building a fort on Sullivan's Island. English ships sail out of Charles Town Harbor.
1776	July 4. Declaration of Independence. Later, four men from South Carolina signed the Declaration.
1776	June 28. English attack fort on Sullivan's Island.
1776	August 2. People of Charles Town get news of the Declaration of Independence.
1780	May 12. English army under General Clinton captures Charlestown.
1782	December 14. The English and Tories leave Charlestown and the American Army takes over the city.

About the Authors:

Susan Dye Lee has been writing professionally since she graduated from college in 1961. Working with the Social Studies Curriculum Center at Northwestern University, she has created course materials in American studies. Ms. Lee has also co-authored a text on Latin America and Canada, written case studies in legal history for the Law in American Society Project, and developed a teacher's guide for tapes that explore women's role in America's past. The writer credits her students for many of her ideas. Currently, she is doing research for her history dissertation on the Women's Christian Temperance Union for Northwestern University. In her free moments, Susan Lee enjoys traveling, playing the piano, and welcoming friends to "Highland Cove," the summer cottage she and her husband, John, share.

John R. Lee enjoys a prolific career as a writer, teacher, and outdoorsman. After receiving his doctorate in social studies at Stanford, Dr. Lee came to Northwestern University's School of Education, where he advises student teachers and directs graduates in training. A versatile writer, Dr. Lee has co-authored the Scott-Foresman social studies textbooks for primary-age children. In addition, he has worked on the production of 50 films and over 100 film-strips. His biographical film on Helen Keller received a 1970 Venice Film Festival award. His college text, *Teaching Social Studies in the Elementary School*, has recently been published. Besides pro-football, Dr. Lee's passion is his Wisconsin cottage, where he likes to shingle leaky roofs, split wood, and go sailing.

About the Artist:

Phillip Shaffer was born in Chicago in 1931. While still in high school, he studied at the Saugatuck School of Painting in Michigan for 2 summers. He won a scholarship to the School of the Art Institute in Chicago and then attended the American Academy of Art.

Mr. Shaffer lives in a suburb with his wife and 3 children and commutes to his Chicago studio each day. In his spare time he paints western landscapes and is represented by a number of galleries in Wyoming.